a small cheese in Provence

cooking with goat cheese

Jean Gill

Jean Gill's previous publications

Novels
One Sixth of a Gill *(The 13th Sign)* 2014
Bladesong *(lulu)* 2012
Song at Dawn *(lulu)* 2011
Someone to Look Up To *(lulu)* 2011
San Fairy Anne *(lulu)* 2010
Crystal Balls *(lulu)* 2010
On the Other Hand *(Dinas)* 2005
Snake on Saturdays *(Gomer)* 2001

Non-fiction
How Blue is My Valley *(lulu)* 2010
A Small Cheese in Provence *(lulu)* 2009
Faithful through Hard Times *(lulu)* 2008
4.5 Years - war memoir - David Taylor *(lulu)* 2008

Poetry
From Bed-time On *(National Poetry Foundation)* 1996
With Double Blade *(National Poetry Foundation)* 1988

Translation (from French)
The Last Love of Edith Piaf - Christie Laume *(Archipel)* 2014
A Pup in Your Life - Michel Hasbrouck 2008
Gentle Dog Training - Michel Hasbrouck *(Souvenir Press)* 2007

Acknowledgements
Special thanks to

Gary Martin – Photo Editor. I asked him for the moon and he gave me the one on p32 plus a cover photo.
Michel Hasbrouck for solving formatting problems
M. Roger Cavet and his family - THE Picodon experts – www.picodon-cavet.fr
Claire Chastan for *Le Picodon – un fromage dans les étoiles*
France Magazine for first publication of features included here
www.picodon-aoc.fr
I have also drawn ideas, inspiration and pleasure in cooking from all of the following:-
Antonio Carluccio, Jamie Oliver, Sophie Grigson, Delia Smith and Robert Carrier.
La Cuisine au fromage de chèvre – Marie Fougère
La cuisine des fromages – Pierrette Chalendar
Fromages a.o.c. de France – l'Association Nationale des Appellations d'Origine Laitières Françaises
Recettes Gourmandes des Boulangers d'Alsace
Gostar la Cuisine Traditionelle de la Drôme et Trièves

and not forgetting my partner in cuisine, who accepted that food had to be photographed before being eaten and who spent many a happy hour discovering that text-boxes have a life of their own.

For my sisters, who also escaped meat and two veg.

Ruth, the Queen of Pastry and Puddings,

and Anne, Juicer Extraordinaire.

As for rosemary, I let it run all over my garden walls, not only because my bees love it, but because it is the herb sacred to remembrance and to friendship, whence a sprig of it has a dumb language.

Sir Thomas More

Contents   Page

Starters/Light Meals

Stars for main courses

Lou chao a empourta lou picaoudou, cha, cha
Lou mangara touou, cha, cha

Oh the cat has got the Picodon, la la…
He'll eat it all in one la la…

The clever cat eats cheese and breathes down rat holes with baited breath.

W. C. Fields

Introduction

Meet 'les chèvres d'ici', the goat cheeses round here (and they are round, here)

FALSE   'chèvre' is a popular French goat cheese

(misinformation in at least one bestselling English cookery book)

TRUE   'chèvre' is French for 'goat' but is also used as a general term for all the cheeses, usually small and round, that are made from goat milk. 'La chèvre' (feminine) is a goat; le chèvre (masculine) is the cheese but 'les chèvres' (plural) could be either.

In Provence, there are many different 'chèvres', some produced entirely by the goat farmers and sold directly at markets and some started on the farms and developed by the 'affineurs', the cheesemakers, from 2/3 day old cheeses. Others are produced by large companies which collect the goat milk and carry out the whole cheese-making process.

Reading the labels

fermier   means that the cheese was made or started by the farmer, using only his or her animals.

laitier   means 'milk producer' and shows which farmer provided the milk to the cheese producer.

Lait cru - good bacteria

The cheese mite has its unexpected fans:

Dead men may envy living mites in cheese,

Or good germs even. Microbes have their joys,

And subdivide, and never come to death.

Wilfred Owen

---

lait cru   unpasteurised milk, considered by cheese lovers to taste better and used by the farmers themselves, so is always a sign of traditional, small-scale cheese-making. Worries about health risks (especially to pregnant women) seem to be contradicted by other studies showing the health benefits of 'good bacteria'

Riddle

Qu'est-ce que ça peut bien être ? Une bête moins grosse qu'une lente devant le roi se faire entendre?

Comment voyage-t-elle? C'est l'artisou qui utilise le Picodon et même le roi connaît sa renommée.

What could it be? A creature smaller than a nit gets a hearing with the king. How does it travel?

It's the cheese mite that travels by Picodon and even the king knows its fame.

---

lait pasteurisé	pasteurised milk, a necessity for the big companies who collect from laitiers, and process the cheese in bigger batches
chèvres chauds	'hot goats' are soft, fresh cheeses ideal for grilling
tomme	any cheese in a rounded shape
crottin	a popular type of goat cheese (see a.o.c.), but sometimes misused to mean 'Chèvre' or any small, round goat cheese. Crottins can be young and creamy or older, drier and stronger.
feuille	the 'feuilles', or leaves, are usually chestnut (as is the case for the a.o.c. Banon), in which some types of chèvre are wrapped to keep them moist
fruitière	a co-operative cheese dairy
a.o.c.	Appellation Contrôlée status has been awarded to the following 12 goat cheeses (so far), protecting the name, region and production method for Banon, Chabichou du Poitou, Chevrotin, Crottin de Chavignol, Pélardon, Picodon, Picodon méthode Dieulefit, Pouligny-Saint-Pierre, Rocamadour, Sainte-Maure de Touraine, Selles-sur-Cher, Valençay.

The Banon is easily recognised by its casing of chestnut leaves but is only truly a Banon when produced in its a.o.c. region, the Vaucluse. Otherwise, however good, it is a copy, a 'chèvre feuille' (goat cheese in leaves). The Picodons are also protected by Appellation Contrôllée status, even stricter for the Prince of Picodons, Picodon mèthode Dieulefit, still produced by the Cavet family, along with the rest of the chèvre family, in Dieulefit ('the village God made'). The Dieulefit Picodon tradition can be traced back to 1367, although the Cavets themselves only lay claim to three generations of cheesemakers, so far ….

Adoun de toun sachou tirei 'no toumo frescho,
A toun crouchou de pan copei 'no lescho

Then you dig in your sack and pull out a fresh cheese,
cut a doorstep of bread and take lunch at ease.

Which goat cheese should you use?

All the recipes in this book have been created with cheeses produced by the Cavet affinerie, Dieulefit, but work with any goat cheese, using the following guidelines. Because Picodons are full-flavoured, I have suggested in the recipes that you replace 1 Picodon with the larger quantity of 100g of another goat cheese.

Age	Les chèvres	Substitute
Youngest	caillé or curds	cottage cheese
	fromage frais	cream cheese
		very soft, melting cheese
Teenage	chèvre chauds	mild, creamy melting cheese
Young adult	tomme or chèvre blanc	mild, more solid cheese
Riper	chèvre crèmeux, feuille,	ripened, drier cheese 'with a sting'
Ripest	Picodon	small cheese, big character
	Picodon mèthode Dieulefit	some old, some new, some blue, mixed with some
Beyond	antique Picodons	eau-de-vie and left to ferment for a month or two.
Surreal	foujou	shoeleather

In general, the youngest goat cheeses are easily sweetened as desserts, the middle-aged are for savouries and the ripest have earned their place on the cheeseboard for their own character. Both middle-aged and ripe chèvres melt in the oven but are often combined with grated gruyère or cheddar to give a traditional gratin appearance. The ancient are tough as old boots and appreciated by those seeking any new sensual experiences, not just good ones. Foujou is for the sort of people who, in the nineteenth century, would have used opium to heighten their creativity.

Foujou
quand las moèichas chèion dau plafon quand dubrètz lo baraston, lo fojon èi bòn per minjar.
When the flies fall off the ceiling if you open the jar, the foujou is ready.

'Steal and Substitute' are the twin pillars of British cuisine; how else would chutney have been invented? So never mind what you're supposed to do, read a recipe, visit the market and have some fun. If the fun is loosely connected to the original recipe and tastes good, then this little book was worth the hours I've spent eating wonderful food in the sunshine – and talking about it.

The poets are mysteriously silent on the subject of cheese.

G K Chesterton

Professional cheese tasters drink only water, but discussion as to how well the wine served complements each cheese – or not - is a far more sociable way of passing the cheese course.

If you want a Provençale ambience with a mild goat cheese, try a well-chilled rosé from that region. Otherwise, the usual choice is a dry white such as Muscadet, Gros Plant or a Haut Savoie de Deux Sèvres for a young goat cheese; Sauvignon, Sancerre or an Ardèchois Viognier for a ripened one.

But what better wine to accompany the robust flavour of a Picodon than its neighbourhood red wine, a Côtes du Rhône Villages from Seguret, Valrèas or Côtes du Ventoux?

Which wine goes with goat cheese?

And with a mixed cheeseboard?

The difficulty is the range of cheeses on the board so that reds such as Gigondas or a St-Emilion, which are superb with Comté, will annihilate Port-Salut.

Traditionally, a selection of cheeses is accompanied by a fruity red, such as a Beaujolais-Villages, a Chinon or young Côtes du Rhône, but a dry white such as a Pouilly-fumé, Côtes du Tricastin, an Alsace Riesling or an Ardèche Chardonnay, make an interesting and increasingly popular alternative. Fortified wines, madeira or a tawny port, are another classic option.

Dans les sentiers pierreux qui mènent à la mer,

Rassasié de thym et de cytise amer,

L'indocile troupeau des chèvres aux poils lisses

De son lait parfumé va remplir les éclisses ;

Charles-Marie Leconte De Lisle (Thestylis)

Along the stony pathways that lead right to the sea

Gorged on thyme and bitter broom

The wayward herd of smooth-haired goats

Take their scented milk to fill the wooden trays

Faute de reculer, leur chute fut commune ;

Toutes deux tombèrent dans l'eau.

Cet accident n'est pas nouveau

Dans le chemin de la Fortune.

Jean de la Fontaine (Les Deux Chèvres)

The Two Goats

So neither gave way and both of them fell

The two of them into the stream

An old, old tale, and you know very well

You should make room for two in your dream.

Which cheeses for your cheeseboard?

Although not all cheese fits neatly into these categories, the table of cheese families is a helpful guide to choosing and storing cheese. When you are buying a selection of cheeses for a cheeseboard, the professional advice is to choose from different categories, with as many cheeses as there are people.

Storing cheese

Anyone who has ever kept a Camembert or Brie a week too long, knows only too well the ooze and smell of an over-ripe soft white cheese, so this is a category to buy carefully. The white rind looks less powdery, more yellow and sunken as the cheese ripens and softens (from the outside in), and the smell strengthens.

Although there are detailed tasting notes available, which score every named variety against its ideal, choosing cheese is still very personal. If you like your Camembert young and firm, don't wait until it is more conventionally ripe – enjoy it now. Soft white cheeses are the most sensitive to storage conditions so are best eaten within a week and kept wrapped in waxed paper in the vegetable drawer of a fridge – unless you are lucky enough to have a 'cave' or cellar.

Ideal storage conditions for cheese are humid, cool and covered, so terracotta containers, waxed paper, (or failing that, clingfilm, preferably only on cut edges, leaving the rind to breathe) and moistened teatowels can all be used to prevent any cheese developing past its best or even growing a mould to turn an Emmental into a Roquefort wanna-be. Big pieces of cheese keep better than small ones but a fortnight is long enough to keep any cheese that was sold ready for eating.

The Seven Classic Families

Le fromage	Type of cheese	Typical Appearance
à pâte fraîche (fromage frais, roulé, cottage cheese)	cream cheese, cottage cheese	creamy or lumpy with curds, no rind, can be spooned or spread
à pâte molle et à croûte fleurie (Camembert, Brie)	soft white cheese	small or medium cheese, usually round, covered in white 'bloom'
à croûte lavée (Munster, Pont l'évêque)	washed rind	reddish rind, slightly rubbery texture
à pâte persillée (Roquefort, bleu d'Auvergne, Stilton	blue cheese	blue veins through cheese
à pâte pressée non cuite (Cantal, Port-Salut, Cheddar)	pressed cheese	small cheeses, dense, slightly rubbery texture
à pâte pressée cuite (Emmental, Gruyère, Ossau-Iraty)	hard cheese (pressed, made from scalded milk)	very large, dense cheeses, some types with holes
de chèvre et de brebis (Picodon, Banon, local varieties	goat and sheep cheese	often very small cheeses, soft rinds sometimes dusted with herbs or spices

Travelling merchants of the old proud breed,

true to their line and selling cheeses

noted my tastes along with other topics

and brought me gifts, each better than the one before.

For me, vast herds had whitened fields and hills,

A thousand goats had wandered, clinging to the cliffs.

Des cocotiers enfin la race antique et fière,

Montrant au-dessus d'eux sa tête tout entière,

Comme autant de sujets attentifs à mes goûts,

Me portaient à l'envi les tributs les plus doux.

Pour moi d'épais troupeaux blanchissaient les campagnes ;

Mille chevreaux erraient suspendus aux montagnes ;

Antoine de Bertin (Elégie)

Perfect Cheese-Cutting

As the old folk tale tells, a man didn't know which of three sisters to choose to be his wife so he asked each of them to cut him a piece of cheese. One pared it; 'Too mean' he said. The second cut a great chunk; 'Extravagant', he said. The third cut a piece not too thin, not too thick; 'Just right', he pronounced and married her.

If you want your cheese-cutting skills to pass a modern spouse test, it's not just the size of the piece that counts; a portion of cheese should always include the range of outer and inner flavours present, so should be cut according to the shape (lengthwise or a wedge from a small round), and include some rind.

Big Franglais Breakfast

Serves 4

preparation time   *10 mins plus 30 mins standing for galette batter*
cooking time   *15 mins*

4 rounds or slices of bacon
4 eggs
8 mushrooms
4 tomatoes
½ Cavet Picodon/50 g goat cheese

Galettes
100g Breton black 'saracen' flour or wholemeal flour
45g plain flour/type 55
1 egg, beaten
25cl water
1tbspn clarified butter (see cook's tip)

Make the batter for the 'galettes' (Breton savoury crepes or pancakes) by sifting the flours with the salt into a mixing bowl. Make a well in the flour, add a little of the water and whisk the beaten egg into the mixture, gradually adding the rest of the water. It is really important to leave the batter to rest at room temperature for 30 minutes. If you have to leave it longer, cover it and chill it. If you are impatient, the galettes will break up like angry popadoms when you try to make pancakes.

Grill the bacon, sliced mushrooms and tomato halves while cooking the galettes. To cook the galettes, use a pancake or frying pan on moderate heat. Add a little clarified butter to the pan and when it sizzles, pour in about three tablespoons of batter or enough to coat the pan in a thick circle. Cook for a minute, or until the pancake is solid, then flip the pancake onto the other side just to seal it. Add more water to the batter if necessary and adjust the heat according to how well the first pancake turned out – the tradition of 'one for the dog' is well-established. Keep the galettes warm, stacked on a plate in the oven

In a separate pan, fry an egg and when it is nearly cooked, put a galette back in the pancake pan, lighter side down, crumble, grate or squidge the goat cheese (depending on its ripeness) onto the galette, and put the fried egg on the top. Fold the galette in two like an omelette and repeat the procedure with the other galettes. Serve with bacon, tomato halves and mushrooms.

conseil d'ami - cook's tip

To clarify butter, melt it in a saucepan over low heat until it separates. You're supposed to let it cool to tepid and pour it into a small bowl, leaving the milky sediments in the pan, but I never bother. For some chemical reason, it is the best pan-grease, better than sunflower oil, which in turn is much better than olive oil.

The traditional method is to cook the egg on top of the galette; replace a galette in the frying pan, uncooked side down, break the egg onto the galette and let it cook through the galette. This is fun but difficult!

Unless your timing is miraculous, it's useful to keep the various foods warm in a low oven until they are all ready. Galettes don't freeze well so if you want ready-made pancakes, but not bought ones, use a recipe with egg, plain flour and milk to make pancakes in advance (e.g. recipe p66), freeze them and reheat last minute in a microwave.

Laughter is brightest
where food is best.

Irish Proverb

Picodon Teasers

Serves 4
preparation time   **20 mins**   **plus 4+hrs marinade**
cooking time   **5 mins**

4 Cavet Picodons/ 400g goat cheese
dry white wine
breadcrumbs
beaten egg

Cut each Picodon into 4 wedges and marinade each wedge in white wine for at least four hours. Roll each wedge in beaten egg and breadcrumbs then deep fry in hot fat for two minutes or until golden.

The fat should be hot enough to turn a bread-cube golden in one minute.

Variation with Batter
250g plain flour / type 55
4 tblspns warm oil
5cl tepid water
4 whites of egg, beaten until stiff
salt

Prepare the batter by sifting the flour into a bowl. Make a well in the flour, add a pinch of salt, the oil and, a little at a time, the water.

Mix it well and when you are ready to use the batter, fold in the egg white. Dip each cheese in the batter and deep-fry as above.

conseil d'ami - cook's tip

Serve with tomato sauce, cranberry sauce or mayonnaise – or all of them.

You can use the cheesy wine marinade in the sauce for ravioli gratin (p(52) or in a bread dough.

Try grape juice, cider or water and herbs instead of the wine marinade.

Then all around from far away across the world he smelled good things
to eat so he gave up being king of where the wild things are.

Maurice Sendak (Where the wild things are)

Lemon Picodon

Serves 4
preparation time   15 mins   and 1+hr to stand

a beardless kiss
has less flavour
than a Picodon without salt

Un poutou s'en barbo
a pas maî de goût
qu'un picaoudou sans soesir.

3 Cavet Picodons / 300g goat cheese
4 tbspns crème fraiche
1 lemon (grated rind and up to 1tbspn juice)
1 small red chili pepper, de-seeded
3 tbspns extra virgin olive oil
1 tbspn fresh oregano leaves
 salt and pepper

Slice the cheese and arrange on a platter. Spread the crème fraiche over the cheese. Grate the rind of the lemon evenly on the crème fraiche, then squeeze half a lemon over the dish, followed by very finely diced chili pepper. Sprinkle the fresh oregano leaves on top, season with salt and pepper. and drizzle the olive oil over the whole topping. Leave for at least an hour in a cool place so that the flavours develop.

conseil d'ami - cook's tip

Be sparing with the lemon juice and chili and add more according to taste. To test the heat of the chili before adding it, try licking your fingernail after chopping the chili – it's a bit less painful than eating a bit of chili!

Leftovers make a good sauce the day after to bake chicken breasts or fish; place the meat or fish in an ovenproof dish, top with the lemon picodon, cover the dish and bake for 30mins at 190° (adjust timings for whatever fish you use).

Je rencontre parfois sur la roche hideuse
Un doux être ; quinze ans, yeux bleus, pieds nus, gardeuse
De chèvres, habitant, au fond d'un ravin noir,
Un vieux chaume croulant qui s'étoile le soir.
J'entends encore au loin dans la plaine ouvrière
Chanter derrière moi la douce chevrière.

Victor Hugo (Pasteurs et troupeaux)

Sometimes on a barren rock I meet
A sweet thing - fifteen, blue eyes, barefoot goatherd
She lives deep in the blackest cleft
In an old thatched house that lights the sky at night.
I still can hear, however far away,
The sweet goatherd's song from
The valley's working day.

Toasts

These spreads make a very tasty combination with slices of goat cheese, especially Picodon méthode Dieulefit, either on crackers or French-style break-your-teeth small toasts.

Dried tomatoes, peppers, aubergines and mushrooms can be bought relatively cheaply in Mediterranean markets, keep very well for a year, are light to carry and travel well if you need to stock up away from home

Tomato caviar

A man taking basil from a woman will love her always.   Sir Thomas More

Makes approx 25cl spread, keeps for 3 weeks in the fridge
preparation time   10 mins, plus ½ hr soaking

15 dried tomatoes
1 teaspoon chopped basil
4 tblspns extra virgin olive oil
small amount (about 1 tspn) Cavet chèvre crèmeux/ mild goat cheese
1 garlic clove

Soak the dried tomatoes for ½ hr in water that has just boiled, then drain. Put the tomatoes, basil, garlic and goat's cheese in a food processor and blend, then add extra oil and blend again until the mixture is a thick paste.

The flavours will mellow after a few days.

conseil d'ami - cook's tip

This recipe came from a marketstall-holder in Nyons, after I became addicted to her tomato caviar and wanted it available in between occasional trips to the Thursday morning market. Her secret is to add a little goat cheese, or mozarella, to mellow the tomato flavour. She also uses her own top quality sundried tomatoes so I bought a kilo. As 15 tomatoes weigh about 60g, a kilo should last a while!

If you're out of basil and need a fix, substitute fresh marjoram,oregano or thyme – or a tiny amount of dried herbes de Provence.

Bachelor's fare : bread and cheese, and kisses.

Jonathan Swift

Tapenade

Makes approx 50cl, keeps up to 3 weeks in the fridge.
preparation time   10 mins

250g olives, stoned –
green olives will make a milder tapenade
6 anchovy fillets, drained of oil
50g capers
1 tbspn/ 60ml extra virgin olive oil
1 garlic clove, peeled
black pepper

Put the olives, anchovies, capers, garlic and oil in a food processor and blend them to a paste. Season to taste with black pepper. You can adjust the flavours to suit yourself by adding more capers, more anchovies, more garlic or more oil.

Pepper Paste

Makes approx 25cl spread, keeps for 3 weeks in the fridge
preparation time   25 mins, plus 1 hr soaking

15 dried red peppers
1 garlic clove
1 shallot
¼ tspn herbes de provence
4 tbspns extra virgin olive oil
2 tbspns water

Soak the dried peppers for an hour or more in water that has just boiled. Remove the peppers with a slotted spoon and rinse them thoroughly as they are very salty. Put the drained peppers with the garlic, shallot, herbs and olive oil in a food processor and blend to a coarse paste.

Simmer the paste in a covered saucepan, with enough water added to prevent sticking, on the lowest possibleheat, for about twenty minutes.

We must love. As tuna loves the salty sea

as swallows air, or goats the yellow broom

or blunt-nosed bees the meadow flowers

Just one kiss from your lips, for me.

Il faut aimer. Le thon aime les flots salés,

L'air plaît à l'hirondelle, et le cytise aux chèvres,

Et l'abeille camuse aime la fleur des blés.

Pour moi, rien n'est meilleur qu'un baiser de ses lèvres.

Charles-Marie Leconte De Lisle (Péristèris)

Aubergine Spread

Makes approx 40cl, keeps up to 3 weeks in the fridge
preparation time   25 mins, plus 1hr soaking

6 strips dried aubergine
1 garlic clove
1 shallot
¼ tspn cinammon
¼ tspn 5 spices
4 tbspns extra virgin olive oil
about 25cl soaking liquid

Soak the aubergine strips for an hour or more in water that has just boiled, then drain them, reserving the soaking liquid. Put the drained aubergines with the garlic, shallot, spices and olive oil in a food processor and blend to a coarse paste.

Simmer the paste in a covered saucepan, with about 25cl of the soaking liquid, on the lowest possible heat, for about twenty minutes or until the paste is soft.

Stir occasionally and add a little soaking liquid if necessary to prevent sticking. If the paste is ready but too runny, remove the lid and reduce the liquid by heating the mixture rapidly while stirring.

Can be used in Courgettes à l'Imam p37.

conseil d'ami - cook's tip

This dip has a very cool, mild flavour that is a good background to fresh parsley or coriander added last minute. For extra oomph, add finely chopped chilli pepper to the mix.

The liquid from soaking dried tomatoes, aubergines, mushrooms or peppers adds flavour to rice, lentils or a bread recipe but don't add salt if you use the pepper water.

Tapenade tip

According to an olive producer in Nyons, top quality olives such as his a.o.c. Tanche olives can be pureed to make tapenade with the addition of only a little herbes de provence and optional garlic – no capers and no anchovies.

Per faïro la biasso

Aven lou saucissou

La bounno omelette

Et lou picaïdou

If you want a good party

you need saucisson

a good omelette

and a Picodon.

Stuffed Tomatoes

Serves 4
preparation time   15 mins   *cooking time   10 mins*

1 Cavet chèvre crèmeux/100g goat cheese
7 large basil leaves, chopped
1 tbspn fromage blanc (or cottage cheese or natural fromage frais or yoghurt)
1 tspn extra virgin olive oil
4 tomatoes
salt and pepper

The night before, mix together the cheeses, the chopped basil, the olive oil, salt and pepper.

On the day, cut off the top of each tomato and keep this to cap the stuffed tomatoes. Hollow out the tomatoes and fill them with the cheese mixture. Serve with a salad in an olive oil dressing.

In Italian the word 'pomodore' for tomato means 'golden apple' so, in several classical myths, perhaps it wasn't apples that lured the hero but tomatoes…

The old name for tomatoes in several languages, including English, was 'love apples'.
afalau cariad (Welsh)
pommes d'amour (French)

conseil d'ami - cook's tip

Instead of throwing them away, you can use the chopped tomato bits and juice as part of the liquid in bread dough, or in the cooking liquid for rice or lentils.

Any fresh herbs work well in this recipe; try parsley or coriander leaves.

Quelques buissons gardent encor

Des feuilles jaunes et cassantes

Que le vent âpre et rude mord

Comme font les chèvres grimpantes.

Anna de Noailles (L'hiver)

Yellow broken leaves still cling to bushes

till the wind, like a clambering goat, devours them.

Cheese Truffles

Celui qui reçoit ses amis et ne donne aucun soin personnel au repas qui leur est préparé, n'est pas digne d'avoir des amis.

Anthelme Brillat-Savarin

Someone who has friends round without giving some personal attention to what they're going to eat, doesn't deserve friends.

Serves 4
preparation time   15 mins
(plus the time to make tapenade, if not bought ready-made – Tapenade recipe p23)
4 Cavet chèvres crèmeux
400g goat cheese rolled into balls
200g tapenade
2 endives or a frisé type lettuce

Roll the cheese balls in the tapenade and serve with the endive or lettuce, lightly dressed as the cheese balls are very rich.

conseil d'ami - cook's tip

'Roll' is not how it works for me in practice; it is much messier and more fun. I usually pat the tapenade onto the cheese and it doesn't matter whether I start off with a triangle on a sphere of cheese, the end result is a very rough ball that really does look amazingly like a truffle ,

As well as making a perfect blend of flavours, losing all hint of bitterness, an endive makes a very useful plate for a cheese truffle – great party food.

Pensant vous délasser d'un tourment inconnu
Qui vous venait des champs, des feuilles, de la terre,
Vous avez sans prudence attaché vos bras nus
Au cou du chevrier dont l'étreinte est amère ;

Anna de Noailles (Bitto)

You hoped you would ease those black thoughts,
the darkness of fields, of leaves, of earth
and you threw your bare arms, reckless
round the goatherd, mistaking his worth.

Omelette Minto

Serves 1
preparation time   5 mins   cooking time   5 mins

for 1 omelette

10g butter
2 mint leaves, chopped
2 eggs
¼ C'avet chèvre crèmeux / 25g goat cheese, crumbled
½ tbspn crème fraiche
salt

Beat the eggs in a bowl. Add the crème fraiche and a pinch of salt, and beat into the egg mixture. Melt the butter in a frying pan, add the chopped mint leaves, then, when the butter is foaming, add the egg mixture, followed at once by the cheese, crumbled over the omelette. Let the omelette set for a minute, then tip the pan back and forward. Loosen the sides of the omelette with a spatula and let any liquid run underneath to set. When the omelette is set, fold it in two or three and serve.

conseil d'ami - cook's tip

For a fluffier omelette, take the pan off the heat when the omelette is nearly set and put it under a preheated grill for a minute (being careful not to burn the handle!) When the omelette has risen, take the pan out from under the grill, fold the omelette and serve. This might not be traditional cuisine but it works really well with a double quantity of omelette mix, which you can then fold, cut into two and serve, avoiding the delay between omelettes.

Add 1 tspn sugar instead of salt to the beaten egg, and serve as a dessert. For this sweet alternative, you could also replace the mint with orangeflower water.

Some words to the moon

Moon
when evening drinks at navy pools
and lays you in the grass
what troubles you ? what hidden urge
disturbs your cool view ?

- I've seen the billy goat, the buck
and his willing, rolling she
mate in the bright night, waking heaven
with their noisy … act.

It's like seeing Daphnis
reach his ready Chloe,
nothing in his way,
it's the smell of love
that shakes the moon.

Paroles à la lune

Ô lune qui le soir venez boire aux étangs
Et vous coucher dans l'herbe,
Quel mal a pu troubler, d'un désir haletant,
Votre langueur superbe ?

- C'est d'avoir vu le bouc irrévérencieux
Et la chèvre amoureuse
S'unir dans la nuit claire, et réveiller les cieux
De leur clameur heureuse ;

C'est d'avoir vu Daphnis s'approcher sans détour
De Chloé favorable...
C'est de sentir monter cette odeur de l'amour,
Ô lune inviolable !

Anna de Noailles

Grilled goat cheese

Serves 4
 preparation time   10 mins   cooking time   5mins

4 slices bread, toasted on one side
4 Cavet chèvres chauds/ 300g goat cheese
1 garlic clove, finely chopped
4 tbspns extra virgin olive oil

Wash and dry the salad leaves and divide them between four plates. Simmer the garlic in olive oil until soft and golden. While the garlic is simmering, spoon the cheese onto the untoasted sides of the slices of bread, leaving a margin of bread uncovered. Place under a hot grill until the cheese is melted and bubbling, and the edges of the bread are golden.

Put one toast on each plate, pour the warm garlic and olive oil over the toast and also drizzle this as a dressing over the salad leaves.

conseil d'ami - cook's tip

It seems that every restaurant in Provence Serves a variation of 'chèvre chaud'. These are sometimes little more than warmed cheeses, sometimes more like British-style cheese on toast in appearance. The essential ingredient is a small, young, fresh goat cheese which, when warmed, will soak up the olive oil and any herbs, whether or not it keeps its shape.

Vary the taste by adding different herbs or spices to the oil dressing; savory or toasted cumin seeds combine well with the cheese. The salad leaves also change the flavour; the more bitter frisé lettuces, oak-leaf and rocket, complement the sweetness of the warm cheese

Tant gratte chèvre que mal gît.

Francois Villon (Ballade des proverbes)

The goat scratches most that beds worst

Courgettes à l'Imam

The aubergine filling is a variation on classic 'Imam bayildi', a stuffed aubergine recipe so delicious that 'the Imam fainted' (at least we assume that it was with pleasure…)

Serves 4
preparation time 20 mins   cooking time   20 mins at 190°

1 small courgette per person
1 portion aubergine spread (see p25)
1 egg
1 Cavet Picodon / 100g goat cheese, crumbled
1 tomato, skinned and de-seeded (see cook's tip p39)
1 tbsn extra virgin olive oil
about 5 slices of bread, crumbed, or 750g breadcrumbs

Poach the courgettes for 1 minute in boiling, salted water, then scoop out and discard the interiors, leaving a thin shell of courgette flesh. Mix all the ingredients in a bowl, sauté them in extra virgin olive oil for a minute and season to taste.

Stuff the courgettes with the mixture and top with breadcrumbs and some knobs of butter. Grease an ovenproof dish and bake the stuffed courgettes in it, covered with aluminium foil, for 20 minutes at 190°.

Remove the foil for about ten minutes to allow the breadcrumbs to go golden brown.

conseil d'ami - cook's tip

You can vary the stuffing by adding cooked rice or ham. You can also add bacon (or French lardons) or minced meat if you sauté it first until well browned (about 5 minutes), then add the other ingredients to the pan and continue as before.

Au mois d'Avril, la chèvre rit

In the month of April, the goat laughs

Picodon crackers

Serves 4
preparation time   15 mins   *cooking time   20 mins at 190°*

2 Cavet Picodons/ 200g goat cheese
16 Nyons olives (or black olives)
4 leaves bought filo pastry
melted butter

Put the leaves of pastry on top of each other, without removing the paper and cut out circles of 30cm, through all the layers. Cut up the Picodons into small chunks, and stone and chop the olives.

Put one pastry circle on a floured worktop and brush it with melted butter. Put a few chunks of cheese and some chopped olives onto the pastry, in the middle of the lower part of the circle, and roll up the pastry into a tube. Pinch the pastry closed around the filling, to make a cracker shape.

Bake in an oven preheated to 190° for 20 minutes.

conseil d'ami - cook's tip

This is my variation of an entrée served in Restaurant la Barigoule, Dieulefit, where Mme Villatte and her son, the Chef de Cuisine, always include local ingredients in the menu and whose cheeseboard will always boast some Picodons.

If you've accidentally poked your finger through the filo pastry and made a hole in the filled section, just cut another circle of filo pastry, brush it with melted butter and wrap it around the first cracker, pinching the ends in exactly the same way. The pastry is so thin that a second leaf won't spoil the cracker at all.

In France, I learned about wine and cheese.

Walter Wager

Roast Tomato and Picodon salad

Serves 4
preparation time   20 mins   plus 12hrs marinade   cooking time   5 mins at 220°

2 Cavet Picodons, each cut into four wedges / 200g goat cheese cut
* into bite-size pieces*
4 small tomatoes
about 1 tbspn extra virgin olive oil
1tspn balsamic vinegar
4 slices of a fresh fennel bulb or four endive leaves
1 sprig of rosemary, 1 bay leaf, black pepper, salt

Marinade the eight wedges of Picodon in enough olive oil to coat them, add pepper and leave overnight in a cold place. Turn them occasionally during the day.

Put the tomatoes in a roasting pan, with the rosemary, bay leaf and a pinch of salt, and drizzle virgin olive oil over them.

Roast the tomatoes for five minutes in an oven preheated to 220°. Cook the fennel or endives in salty boiling water for four minutes, then drain. Sprinkle the balsamic vinegar over the sizzling hot tomatoes the moment you bring them out of the oven and share out the tomatoes, the cheese wedges and the fennel, spooning all the pan juices over everything. Serve warm.

conseil d'ami - cook's tip

If you use a fennel bulb, reserve the leaves for edible decoration and don't cut off the base until after the slices have cooked – they will keep their shape better.

Any green salad combination will work with the oils from the picodon and the tomatoes added last minute as a dressing.

To skin and de-seed a tomato, put the tomatoes into a saucepan and pour boiling water over them so that they are covered. Leave them for one minute, scoop them out with a slotted spoon and make two score marks down the length of each tomato with a sharp knife. When the tomatoes are cool enough, peel off the skin, cut each tomato in half and squeeze up the seeds, discarding these and keeping the flesh. Leftover salsa tastes good with burgers or pork chops.

… while, on a side plate, goat cheeses the size of a child's fist, hard and grey, look like the pebbles rolled around the bends of stony paths by billy goats leading their herds.

...tandis que, dans un plat à côté, des fromages de chèvre, gros comme un poing d'enfant, durs et grisâtre, rappelaient les cailloux que les boucs, menant leur troupeau, font rouler aux coudes des sentiers pierreux.

Emile Zola (Le Ventre de Paris)

Chicken Pic-pockets

Serves 4
preparation time   20 mins   *cooking time   30 mins at 190°.*

4 chicken breasts, slit lengthwise to form pockets
I Cavet Picodon/ 100g goat cheese
½ tspn dried herbes de Provence
salt and pepper

Preheat the oven to 190°. Place the four chicken breasts on a roasting tray. Cut the Picodon into four wedges, then roughly cut up each wedge and squash the pieces into the chicken pocket. Sprinkle the herbs and seasoning into the pocket, then flatten it shut. Cover the tray with aluminium foil and bake for 30 minutes at 190°.

conseil d'ami - cook's tip

Replace the herbes de Provence with paprika or chopped sage

Snippets of ham, mushrooms or reconstituted sun-dried tomatoes are also tasty variations added to the cheese.

Arcadian goat-footed Pan,
helmeted with two horns,
loud and loved by shepherds…

Pan d'Arcadie, aux pieds de chèvre, au front armé
De deux cornes, bruyant, et des pasteurs aimé…

Charles-Marie Leconte De Lisle (Pan)

Courgette Crumble

Serves 4
preparation time   15 mins   cooking time   30 mins at 190°

400g courgettes (preferably small, young and firm – forget equal opportunities)
2 Cavet chèvres crèmeux/ 200g goat cheese
1 tbspn mint leaves, chopped
50g walnuts
approx 5 slices of bread reduced to crumbs/ 75g breadcrumbs
2 tbsns extra virgin olive oil (or chips of butter/cooking margarine)
salt and pepper

Grate the courgette and leave it in a sieve to drain for fifteen minutes or more. Squeeze out the excess liquid before combining the courgette with the goat's cheese, mint and seasoning in a gratin dish.

Chop the walnuts finely, add to the breadcrumbs and then stir in the olive oil.
Spread the nut crumb topping over the courgette mix and bake for 30 minutes at 190°.

conseil d'ami - cook's tip

If you think the courgettes might be old and bitter (it happens to the best of us) add a little salt to them while they are grated and draining.

If the top has browned too quickly, cover the bake with metal foil or a lid and continue cooking. This works for any bake.

Pizza Gallois

Are the 'Gallois', Welsh people, really turophiles? I certainly am.

There was an English belief in Shakespeare's day that the Welsh loved cheese, especially toasted of course. This was supposedly a sign of barbarian habits and used for Welsh jokes of much the kind the French use about English 'rosbifs'

'I will rather trust a Fleming with my butter, Parson Hugh the Welshman with my cheese, an Irishman with my aqua-vitae bottle than my wife with herself...

God defend me from that Welsh fairy lest he transform me to a piece of cheese.'
(The 'Welsh fairy' is Sir Hugh Evans, who is disguised as a satyr at the time).

William Shakespeare (The Merry Wives of Windsor)

Serves 4
preparation Time   *for pizza base (with rising time) 1 ½ hrs*
                               for topping   *20 mins*
Cooking Time   *20 mins at 200*

Pizza Base – if you want to make one, try this …

325g oz plain flour / type 55
2 tbspns extra virgin olive oil/ 25g butter/cooking
margarine, melted
1large egg
15 cl milk
1½ tspns ready to use dried yeast
1tspn salt
2 tspns sugar

Measure the flour into a big bowl then sprinkle the yeast into the flour. Beat the egg, make a well in the flour and add all the liquids. Use a wooden spoon, then your hands to mix the dough and when it is firm, take the dough out of the bowl and knead it firmly for 5-10mins until it is bread dough consistency. If it is too sticky to knead, add more flour and if it is too dry, add a little milk.

When the dough is smooth and elastic, put it in a bowl, in warm place, cover it with cling film and leave it to rise for about an hour until roughly doubled in size. Knock it back down on the worksurface, then shape it into a round (approx 10inches in diameter), or a rectangle on a pizza or baking tray.

After about ½ hour the base will have risen again and will be ready for topping and cooking.

If you have a breadmaker, throw the ingredients into the breadpan and make the dough on the pizza setting (or stop before baking). The dough is now ready to be shaped into a pizza – or of course, lots of little ones.

conseil d'ami - cook's tip

I shape the dough by bashing it with the heel of my hand but if you're less aggressive you can use a rolling-pin.

Thin baking trays with no lip on three sides conduct heat well, crisp the base and make it easy to serve slices of pizza when it's cooked.

Pizza Topping

1 large leek
100g chopped walnuts
1 Cavet Picodon / 100g goat cheese
2 tbspns extra virgin olive oil
salt and pepper

Wash and clean the leek by removing tough outer leaves and any discoloured green parts, slicing off the top and bottom, and rinsing it along a lengthwise cut to get any earth out of the layers. Dry and finely grate the leek (white and green parts), then sauté it gently in the hot oil, not browning it, until it is completely softened. Add salt to taste and leave the leek to cool.

When the pizza base is ready, spread the cooled leek and extra virgin olive oil mix evenly to within ½ cm of the edges. Drip the last drops of flavoured oil onto the pizza – don't waste them.

Now it's time to be arty; make a pattern with the chopped walnuts – spirals, blobs, criss-cross – then thinly slice the goat's cheese and add that to your work of art. I plan my pattern and subdivide the portions of nuts and goat's cheese before I start (or cheat and get some more out of the cupboard in the interests of symmetry).

Then bake your pizza for 15/20 minutes at 200°. If the dough edges are brown and the cheese melting and showing brown spots, the pizza is cooked.

conseil d'ami - cook's tip

If you use walnuts in the pizza, try walnut oil in a vinaigrette salad dressing to serve with it. For a quick, simple dressing, I use 1 part vinegar to 6 parts oil, with a little salt, and either blend them with a fork or shake them in the serving bottle. If I use a fancy vinegar like lavender or redcurrant, I use plain olive oil; if I use a fancy oil, I use a white or red wine vinegar, or lemon juice. I leave out the mustard so often recommended in recipes because I like to taste the oil and vinegar.

Different pizza toppings combine well with the basic leek and goat cheese. Sliced mushrooms, sweet peppers, pine nuts instead of walnuts, and tomato rings all work well.

Pour patrimoine il a sept chèvres;

Quand l'air de l'aube en ses poumons

Vibre, on le voit passer par monts

Comme un bon dieu la flûte aux lèvres.

Emile Nelligan (Pan moderne)

A Modern Pan
Seven goats his legacy
And when the morning air strums
His lungs, you see him stride the hills
Godlike, as, with flute he comes.

50

Potato Galettes

Serves 2
preparation time 20 mins   *cooking time*   *15 mins*

1 Cavet Picodon / 100g goat cheese, grated
300g potatoes
2 beaten eggs
2 tbspns crème fraiche
2 tbspns plain flour /type 55
1tbspn clarified butter (see p15)
salt and pepper

Peel and boil the potatoes until soft enough to mash. Mix in the crème fraiche while mashing the potatoes, season with salt and pepper then leave the mixture to chill for an hour. Add the beaten eggs and the flour to the mixture, combining the ingredients without over beating. Finally, add the grated Picodon.

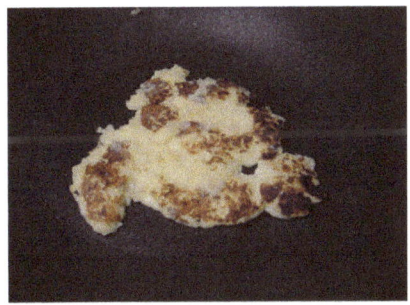

Heat a tablespoon of clarified butter in a frying pan, then add a ladleful of mixture and allow this to brown before turning it with a spatula

When it is brown on both sides, remove the galette and keep it warm until the stack of galettes is ready to serve.

conseil d'ami - cook's tip

A really good non-stick pan makes a big difference to successful galettes; the first time I achieved anything other than a burnt pan-bottom was with a non-stick flat-bottomed wok. Galette mix, like pancake batter, has an alternative life as wallpaper paste.

Splodges of mixture can be flattened, broken up, turned, squidged and treated quite roughly. Think handmade, tustic cloud shapes rather than neat rounds.

Leek and potato bake

Serves 4
preparation time   20 mins   *cooking time   40 mins at 180°*

1 leek, prepared as for the Pizza Gallois (p46)
4 large baking potatoes/ 800g potatoes, peeled
2 Cavet chèvres crèmeux / 200g goat cheese
100g crème fraiche
10cl milk
salt and pepper
butter

Finely slice the leek into a bowl. Then finely slice the potatoes into another bowl. Grease an ovenproof dish and line it with a layer of potatoes. Crumble about a quarter of the cheese over the potatoes and add a little salt and pepper.

Next, add a layer of leek slices and crumble another quarter of the cheese over these. Repeat these layers and finish with a layer of potatoes. If there is any cheese left, crumble this over the top.

Then spread the crème fraîche evenly over the potatoes, pour the milk over the bake, season lightly and top with some tiny knobs of butter. Bake in an oven pre-heated to 180° for up to 40 minutes or until a knife-point slides easily through the leek and potato slices.

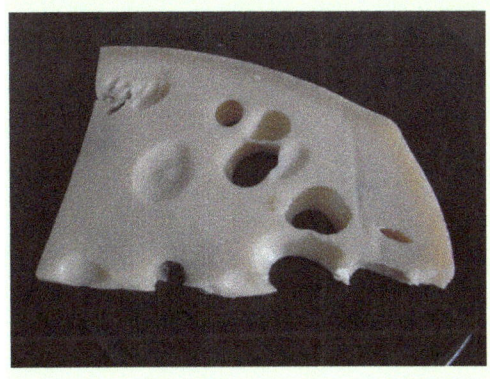

What makes the holes in Emmental or any type of Gruyère?

At a slightly higher temperature than for other 'pâte cuite' cheeses a germ ferments, creating bubbles of carbon dioxide gas that become the holes that you see.

Printemps

Rameau vert du Passeur ou branche qu'apporta
La colombe de l'Arche, ah ! la verte saveur
Du buisson que tondra la chèvre aux yeux rêveurs !

Etre chèvre sans corde, éblouie à ce tas
De bourgeons lumineux qui mettent un halo
Sur la campagne verte - aller droit devant soi
Dans le bruit de grelots
Du ruisseau vagabond - suivre n'importe quoi,
Sauter absurdement, pour sauter - rire au vent
Pour l'unique raison de rire... Comme Avant !

Premieres feuilles
Petits doigts en coquilles,
Petits doigts jeunes, lumineux, pressés de vivre,
Par-dessus les vieux murs vous vous tendez vers nous.
Le vieux mur dit : " Gare au vent fou,
Gare au soleil trop vif, gare aux nuits qui scintillent,
Gare à la chèvre, à la chenille,
Gare à la vie, ô petits doigts !

Sabine Sicaud

Springtime

Green branch for the Ferryman or for the dove
that brought peace to the Ark, ah! The green taste
of bushes clipped by dreaming goats.

To be a goat, untethered, dazzled by the wealth
of gleaming buds, a shining halo
greening over fields – to head straight
among the tinkling bells
into the wandering stream;
to follow each new whim
to skitter sideways only for the dance
to laugh into the wind
for nothing but the laughter… Like Before!

First leaves
little fingers all in shells
children's fingers green with gleaming life
leaning on old walls towards us.
The old wall murmurs, 'Beware the mad wind,
beware the sun's glare and the dazzling night
beware the goat and the caterpillar,
beware life itself, little fingers of green.

Ravioli Gratin

Serves 4
preparation time   15 mins   *cooking time   10 mins at 180°*

ravioli (180g per person)
25cl Clairette de Die/ sparkling or any dry white wine
25cl crème fraiche
½ Cavet Picodon/ 50g goat cheese
two slices streaky bacon, cut into halves
oil
2 shallots
salt and pepper

Make the sauce by gently frying the shallots in a little oil until translucent and season them.

Add the wine to the shallots, bring it to the boil, then add the crème fraiche and let the sauce reduce over a gentle heat by about half for 8 to 10 minutes.

Boil the ravioli in salted water until al dente, drain it and put the cooked pasta in a gratin dish.

Cover the ravioli with the sauce, add the sliced or crumbled Picodon and streaky bacon. Bake in a preheated oven at 180° for 10 minutes and serve hot with a green salad.

conseil d'ami - cook's tip

You can replace the wine with water for a family meal but make sure you heat the crème fraiche to boiling point first, and preferably add boiling water, or the sauce is likely to curdle.

I like ravioli filled with ham for this dish, with a strong Picodon.

Pòt se dire qu'èi bòn una bèla revuèra!

Cataa d'un det au mens de fromage de gruièra...

Las laissèm pas fregir, mafè, sarià damage.

N'en sòrto de siètas que 'cato fromage.

Nos romprèm pas les dents, car aquì li a gis d'òus;

Anèm, attaqèm las, e n'aièm gis de paur.

Mingèm sens las comptar, e minjèm n'en encara

Vèi donc, si èra manchaa, quèla farià una para.

Leon Eimard (Las Revèras)

You could say it's good, ravioli well made

topped with some gruyère extra thick-laid

Don't let it get cold, now that would be a waste

when there's hot melted cheese all in piles on the plates.

We won't break our teeth 'cos there aren't any bones

so dive in, get cracking, and let's have no moans,

no need to be stingy, there's always some more

so check who has finished – she's guzzled for sure.

A small garden, figs, a little cheese, and, along with this, three or four good friends —such was luxury to Epicurus.

Friedric Nietzsche (A wanderer and his shadow)

Aubergine Soufflé

Serves 4
preparation time   10mins
cooking time   1+hr in advance for the aubergines,
*   then 30 mins at 190° for the soufflé*

1 Cavet Picodon/ 100g goat cheese
3 aubergines, wiped clean
2 eggs
about 40g gruyère or cheddar cheese
salt and pepper

Prick the aubergines with a fork and cook them uncovered in a microwave for 15 minutes, or in an oven preheated to 190° for about ¾ of an hour, or until the aubergine flesh is very soft. If you prod the aubergine, it will feel squidgy like a pillow, when it is ready.

You can do this in advance and let the aubergines cool; if you leave it to the last minute, you will need asbestos hands when you cut the aubergines in two and scrape the flesh into a bowl or a food processor. Either machine-blend, grate or mash the goat cheese into the aubergine, with salt and pepper and parsley. Then add the two eggs, beating them well into the mixture.

Grease a casserole dish and spoon the aubergine mixture into the dish. Grate the gruyère over the top and place the soufflé into the preheated oven to bake at 190° for 30 mins. The soufflé is ready when it has risen well and the top is bubbling and golden brown. Add some fresh parsley to each serving. The texture is soft but set, like a mousse.

conseil d'ami - cook's tip

This tastes really good eaten cold the next day, like a quiche but without the fuss of pastry-making.

Si vous n'êtes capable d'un peu de sorcellerie, ce n'est pas la peine de vous mêler de cuisine.

Colette (le Muscat Treille)

If you can't work a little magic, don't bother trying to cook.

Tarte à Chèvre

Serves 4
preparation time for pastry   10mins to make,   1hr to chill,   5mins to roll out
*   for filling   15mins   30+mins to cool*

shortcrust pastry
250g plain flour
* type 45*
½ tspn salt
125g butter
1 egg

Rub the flour, salt and butter together until the mixture looks like breadcrumbs. Add the egg and work the mixture, first with a fork, then with your hands, until it is a smooth dough, then wrap it in clingfilm and leave it to chill for an hour.

filling
750g onions
2tbspns extra virgin olive oil
100g crème fraiche
1 heaped tbspn cornflour or Maizena
1Cavet chèvre crèmeux/ 100g goat cheese
salt, pepper and about ½ tspn nutmeg

Peel and finely chop the onions then stew them in the oil, in a covered pan, on a low heat, for ten to fifteen minutes until they are very soft. Stir from time to time and don't let them brown.

In a bowl, mix the cream and the flour, then the cheese, mashing it in with a fork. Season this mixture to taste with salt, pepper and nutmeg and spread it over the onions in the frying pan. Bring the whole mixture to boiling point, stirring throughout, then take it off the heat and leave it to cool.

Grease a flan dish (25-30cm in diameter), roll the pastry out and line the dish with it. Prick the pastry lightly with a fork. Spoon the cool filling into the flan and bake for 30mins at 190° or until the filling has set, the pastry edges are light brown and the top is bubbling and golden.

conseil d'ami - cook's tip
Bacon bits or lardons can be sprinkled onto the flan before it is baked to add flavour.

The onion filling freezes well and tastes equally good on a pizza base, or spread on some leftover bread and grilled for a quick snack.

I always fold the pastry in three to put it into the flan dish. Two small flans are easier to roll pastry for and you can eat one hot and one cold.

Ni les chèvres paissant les cytises amers

Aux pentes des proches collines,

Ni les pasteurs chantant sur les flûtes divines,

N'ont troublé la source aux flots clairs.

Charles-Marie Leconte De Lisle (La Source)

Not goats grazing the bitter broom

on the slopes of nearby hills

Nor shepherds playing the pipes of Pan

Disturb the clear spring trills.

Where do the Drômoises go for a Christmas break? Strasbourg of course, the capital of Christmas which smells of mulled wine and spiced cake, where the master bakers of Alsace offer a CD of their songs and their top tips on baking ginger biscuits, Kugelhopf and tarte flambé. Although I resisted the songs, I couldn't resist the recipes and I can't fault the results. Thank you master-bakers, especially for the 'perfect pastry' in this recipe, after many disasters with French flour. What on earth is 55? 45? 65? I had to learn baking by numbers.

Master Bakers' Crèche – made from dough

French supermarket flours

It is easy enough to buy everything in the village boulangeries from a 'multigrain' (granary) to a walnut loaf that is sold by the kilo and must have been baked in an oven the size of the nuclear furnace across the valley. 55 is everyday French flour, similar to basic plain flour but also used as strong plain flour 45 is a more expensive patisserie flour, more finely ground and containing more gluten. 'complète' is wholemeal, which in my experience will produce concrete loaves unless mixed 1:3 with 55, This is also true of 'seigle' (rye), 'mais' (cornmeal) and 'Saracen' or 'Breton noir' which has a nutty flavour and is used for Breton savory pancakes. 'fluide' is a very fine flour which works well in sauces or instead of type 00 for pasta. Maizena is a commercial version of cornflour, popular in sauces and cake-making, and not to be confused with 'farine de mais' which is the yellow cornmeal.

Supermarkets here in the midi are just starting to stock granary flours and I've grown used to adding my own seeds to a complète/ 55 blend; linseed (lin), poppy (pavot) , sesame (sesame), fennel (fenouil), and of course sunflower (tournesol) are all available on market herb stalls. Beware roasted sunflower seeds unless you want to spear your gums. I check that the seeds I buy are the soft type. Some combination standard British spices, such as mixed spice and pickling spice, are also difficult to get here and I make them up from the separate ingredients.

Of course if you live anywhere near the master bakers of Strasbourg, you'll find the granary flours of your seediest dreams…

Salsa

One or more salsas can be made in advance, preferably at least an hour but ideally about 8 hours, and will keep for up to three days. Each salsa Serves 4 people. Combine all the ingredients in a bowl and leave the salsa in the fridge until an hour before serving.

tomato salsa
700g or 4 very large tomatoes, skinned and de-seeded, then finely chopped (see cook's tip p39)
2 shallots, finely chopped
1 green chilli pepper, de-seeded and very finely chopped
juice of 1 lime or ½ lemon
2tbspns fresh coriander leaves chopped, salt and pepper

plum salsa
400g ripe plums
1 shallot
2tbspns fresh coriander leaves chopped
juice of 1 lime or ½ a lemon
1 red chilli pepper, de-seeded and very finely chopped, salt and pepper

fruit salsa
1 ripe avocado, peeled, stoned and finely diced
1 small ripe mango, peeled, stoned and finely diced
½ red onion
2tbspns fresh coriander leaves chopped
juice of 1 lime or ½ a lemon
1 red chilli pepper, de-seeded and very finely chopped
salt and pepper

conseil d'ami - cook's tip

It is the salsa that makes this dish so don't be tempted not to bother. The combination of fresh fruit with chili pepper is like kissing someone who is really reserved and being stunned by the passion in the response.

Try other fruits in the salsa when they are in season and cheap; choose cool, juicy fruit and add chili heat; apricot and melon is interesting. Golden plums add interesting colours.

Parsley, basil and coriander leaves lose most of their taste if cooked and contribute little to the dish; for maximum impact, add some last minute and save some to serve with the food.

The opposite is true of dried herbs and spices – add them at the beginning of the cooking process.

It is trendier – and more like the Latin American tortilla traditions – to use a lime but a lemon works just as well.

Quesadilla

Serves 2   *total cooking time*   *20 mins including 10 mins at 200°*

3 tortillas
1 courgette, cut into matchsticks
1 red pepper, cut into matchsticks
1 shallot, sliced
2 garlic cloves, chopped
2tbsns extra virgin olive oil
about 1tspn balsamic vinegar
1 tbsp fresh coriander leaves, chopped
1 Cavet chèvre crèmeux/ 100g goat cheese
80g grated emmental or cheddar
salt and pepper

Sauté the courgette, shallot and pepper in the oil on a high flame for about 10 minutes, stirring occasionally, until they have brown patches. Add the garlic and sauté for another minute. Straight away, but off the heat, sprinkle the vinegar over the pan, then stir in the coriander, salt and pepper.

Put one tortilla on a baking tray and spread half of the courgette mix on it. Then sprinkle half the goat cheese and half the emmental on top. Place a second tortilla on top of the first and press it down lightly. Repeat the filling and finally lay the third tortilla on top, flattening this gently. Bake the quesadilla for about 8/10 minutes at 200°, until the tortilla has browned, the edges are crisp and the cheese has melted. Serve it with a salsa and a green salad.

Asparagus crèpes

filling
500g fresh asparagus
2 Picodons, cut up into small pieces
grated rind of ½ lemon
3 tbsns crème fraiche
salt and pepper

pancake batter
100g plain flour
2 eggs
1 tbspn olive oil/melted butter
15cl milk
15cl water
pinch of salt

Prepare the filling first; this can be done well in advance. If necessary, wash the asparagus spears, then trim the asparagus by shaving the sides of each stalk with a potato peeler from the tip down to the stem – this will get rid of woody strands. Next, break each one off at the base, where it snaps. Discard these end bits and steam or boil the asparagus for about 15 minutes or until tender, ideally standing the asparagus as a bundle so that the delicate tips are out of the water.

When cool enough to handle, cut the asparagus spears into roughly two centimetre lengths and mix gently with the other filling ingredients. Save 1 tbspn of crème fraiche to garnish the crèpes.

Make the pancake batter by sifting the flour and salt into a bowl. Make a well and add the eggs, oil and a little liquid. Beat until smooth then gradually add the remaining liquid. If possible, leave the batter to stand for half an hour, then make 8 or 9 pancakes. Preheat the oven to 180°C while making the pancakes.

Put a little asparagus mixture onto a pancake and roll it around the filling. Place the crèpes in a shallow baking tray, spread the tbspn of crème fraiche across them, cover the tray with aluminium foil and bake for 20mins. Serve two crèpes per person for a main course, or one for a starter

Asparagus was banned from French convent schools in the past, as a vegetable unsuitable for young ladies…

A chava sur mon ganoux

Annur a la ferma dei Boulou

Lli s'en quatrè lli s'en prou

Purd mangea lou picaoudou

Ride my knee to

the farm of Balou

One and two and three and four

we'll eat our Picodons

and won't need more.

More ideas?

ham cornets – mix a Picodon with some crème fraiche and herbs, put a dollop of this mix on a large slice of ham and roll it up.

lapin gallois – yes, Welsh rabbit (not the mistaken 'rarebit') with goat cheese. Melt a Picodon with a glass of lager (or bière blonde) and a teaspoon of mustard. You can either reduce it to thicken or take it off and carefully add a beaten egg yolk. Don't bring it to boiling point when you reheat.

cheesy salad dressing – crush a creamy goat cheese in a bowl, add three tbspns olive oil, mixing with a fork, then a tbspn lemon juice and some fresh herbs. Try ½ tbspn cider vinegar instead of lemon juice and serve with apple slices, nuts and lettuce.

dip – crush a creamy goat cheese with paprika or garlic and herbs, and serve with celery sticks.

stuffed peppers – cut large sweet peppers into halves lengthwise and remove the stalks. Crush the cheese and mix with beaten eggs, thyme and cinnamon, then stuff the pepper halves with this mixture. Put the peppers in a baking dish, top them with breadcrumbs and add some vegetable stock or water to the baking tray so that the peppers bake in a moist oven for about 20 mins.

prawn picocktail – crush a creamy cheese with 2tbspns crème fraiche, 1tbspn of lemon juice, some grated rind and some tomato puree. Add some cooked prawns and season with paprika, salt and pepper.

stuffed pancakes – blend cooked leeks, mushrooms, eggs and a creamy cheese. Stuff and roll pancakes with the mixture and cook them as a gratin for 5 mins.

old, dry goat cheese can be used like parmesan, grated into soup, onto pasta and pizzas…

chicken stuffing – blend a creamy cheese with a chicken liver, an egg and herbs, to make an unusual but tasty stuffing.

cheeseburgers – mix a crushed cheese with minced beef, lightly fried onions, and an egg, then shape the burgers and grill or fry them.

baked potatoes – bake the potatoes in advance, cut them in halves, scoop out most of the potato leaving lined shells. Mix the potato well with a cheese and some crème fraiche. Fill the shells with this mixture and bake for 10 mins in a hot oven.

pasties – fill shortcrust pastry circles with cheese and apple slices, then bake.

seafood mousse – combine cooked prawns and crabmeat with crushed creamy cheese, some crème fraiche and lemon juice. Season with pepper, put the mixture in a cake tin or mold, cover with clingfilm and leave to chill for at least 5hrs.

stuffed pasta shells – use the huge pasta shells, conchiglioni rigati, boil them until al dente, then stuff each one with a mixture of chopped ham, lightly fried shallots and grated cheese. Top with breadcrumbs to which a little finely chopped garlic and grated gruyère or cheddar has been added, place in a gratin dish and grill for 5 mins.

forgotten bread – put some buttered leftover bread in a gratin dish. Lightly fry some onions and put them on the bread. Crumble the goat cheese in a bowl and add milk a little at a time until the mixture is smooth then beat in a couple of eggs. Cover the bread with this mixture and bake for 30 mins.

merry melons – use one small, ripe melon per person. Make a conical opening at the stalk end, about 4cm deep, and reserve the melon plug you have cut out. Remove seeds with a small spoon, prick the interior with a fork and insert grated Picodon and a small glass of a liqueur, such as chartreuse. Replace the melon stopper and chill the melon for at least 3hrs. Serve with Parma ham.

C'est le temps où la feuille aux ramures déborde,

La montagne nourrit des herbes de senteur,

Notre chèvre s'ennuie et tire sur sa corde

Pour atteindre aux lavandes fines des hauteurs.

Cécile Sauvage (La maison sur la montagne)

In wild and blowy weather
when sweet herbal scents drift by
our goat frets and tugs its tether
to reach true lavender on high

'Entre la poire et le fromage' , 'Between the pear and the cheese'

meaning 'during the dessert course', or when relaxed and comfortable.

Sweet cheese

honeyed chèvre chaud – put a small fresh cheese in a ramekin, add a spoonful of honey and bake for ten minutes in a medium oven.

zapped fromage frais – soak raisins overnight in brandy, cointreau, grand marnier or any other little acoholic weakness, then mix the raisins and alcohol into the fromage frais. Serve chilled.

cheese tart – use sweet pastry, sugar and crème fraiche mixed in the cheese filling and use very young creamy cheese. Top with fresh fruit – cherries, orange slices...

baked pears or apples – core the fruit and replace the cores with a mix of creamy cheese and crème fraiche, flavoured with cinnamon, then bake for about 30 mins.

sweet toast – grill slices of bread on one side, turn them and brush the ungrilled side with olive oil, crumble creamy cheese on top and drizzle honey over the toasts, then grill again for a minute or two.

fruity buns – use plums, peaches, apricots or strawberries in any combination, stoned and cut in two. Reserve some for decoration, and simmer the rest with some sugar until jam-like. Heat brioche type buns in the oven for a few minutes, then hollow each one and fill with creamy cheese. Cover the buns with the jam and a little honey, then place under a low grill for a few minutes. Serve cold.

Vite! Apportez-moi le dessert - je sens que je vais passer

I feel the end approaching. Quick, bring me my dessert, coffee and liqueur.

Last words of Pierrette, the great aunt of Anthelme Brillat-Savarin, eight weeks before her 100th birthday

Et de sa douce main, enfin,
Détache une chèvre qui broute
A san piquet, au bord des routes,
Et doucement la baise et la caresse
Et gentiment la mène en laisse.

Emile Verhaeren (La petit vierge)

The little maiden

with her tender hand at last
untethers the goat that grazes
at her stake beside the road
and with sweet kisses and caresses
leads her gently, without goad.

Picodons, Olives, Garlic – Les Confrèries

The Fête at Saou and Dieulefit's equivalent 'le Picodon chez lui' (the 'chez lui' a defiant reminder that this is the true centre of Picodon production) are opportunities for the Confrèrie of the Picodon, its Guild, to promote the cheese and award their prizes. The Confrères are distinguished by their cream cloaks, trimmed with olive braiding around a layered wrapround neckline. They also wear medallions displaying their insignia, a goat and a ladle, and the last line of 'le Serment du Chevalier', their creed.

Anyone admitted to the Confrèrie must promise:

'Je m'engage à promouvoir et à défendre

en toute occasion et en tout lieu

le Picodon

et fais mienne cette devise

'le Picodon maintiendrons'.

I promise to promote and defend

the Picodon

whenever and wherever I can

and to make this motto my own -

we will support the Picodon

The medallion

Procession in 2007 to launch the 'Picodon Route' and celebrate the new sculptures along the way.

Dieulefit's Picodon goats advertise the village's reputation for music.

The confrères meet and parade at neighbours' fêtes

Wine confrères at the Picodon fête in Saou

The olive Confrérie at their February harvest festival in Nyons

The garlic Confrèrie

Plus vive que la chèvre ou la fière génisse,
Plus blanche que le lait qui caille dans l'éclisse,
O Galatée, ô toi dont la joue et le sein
Sont fermes et luisants comme le vert raisin !
Charles-Marie Leconte De Lisle (Les plaintes du Cyclope)

Livelier than goat or proud heifer
Whiter than milk as it curdles in trays
O Galatea! Your cheeks and your breasts
are rounded and fine like the grapes on the vine

Cheese with a Sting - the story of le Picodon (a.o.c.)

The Picodon is not a cheese, it is a flattened round of history, a taste of home for anyone living in la Drôme or l'Ardèche. The first written reference to the cheese was in 1361, in Dieulefit, which to this day has its own specific a.o.c. for the Prince of Picodons, made by the méthode Dieulefit. In 1367, two unlucky merchants taking their Picodons by donkey-cart to from Dieulefit to market in Montélimar were attacked and their cheeses stolen. Even the name 'Picodon' shows its fine pedigree; there is general agreement that it derives from the local patois 'picau', meaning 'piquant' or 'stinging' the tongue. A good Picodon will do just that and the older the Picodon, especially if it is a Picodon méthode Dieulefit, the stronger its 'sting'.

Bouta la man au tchazeirou
De teasque man un picaoudou

Dip your hand in the bag
and pull out a Picodon in each one

So strong is Picodon nostalgia, that there are letters home from the front in the First World War, thanking mothers and wives for the cheeses they sent. One such notes that the Picodons were 'so good that there is only one left' and the soldier was 'content that Marie is looking after the goats so well and is so sensible and my little Jean too, but I mustn't think of them too much or I will feel terrible.' In his day, it would have been his wife, his mother, or his grandmother, who actually made the Picodon. Goats were 'the cows of the poor' and it was the women who made the goat cheese, handing the recipes down through the family in a purely oral tradition.

It was not only the peasants who missed their Picodons; in the 1890s, when the Montélimar politician M. Emile Loubet became President of France, he organised a weekly consignment of his favourite cheese to be sent to him in Paris. He must have missed the arrival of the marketday train, nicknamed 'le Picodon', which made seventeen stops on its route delivering coal for the wool and silk factories, bricks for the potteries, and Picodons from Dieulefit to

Montélimar market, twenty-eight kilometres away. Nowadays two cats blink at the world from the windowsills of the old, disused station, a toy-town house in the middle of a Dieulefit carpark.

The Picodon also lays claim to being the only cheese to have gone into space, sneaked onto the 1996 NASA Columbia space mission by a Drômoise astronaut and medical specialist. Jean- Jacques Favier defied the US ground laws regarding unpasteurised cheeses to take seventeen Picodons, one for each day of orbit, as part of his personal allowance. Having had Picodons confiscated in the past, the only way he could them past American customs officials was by mailing them to his address in the USA. So popular were the cheeses with the crew of seven, that the astronauts held a reunion at the Picodon Fête at Saou, a traditional annual celebration.

To be called a Picodon, the small round goat's cheese, in the shape of an ice-hockey puck, has to be 45 per cent 'matières grasse' (fat content), from 'lait du chevre entier' (full fat goat's milk) and be 4 to 7 centimetres in diameter and 1.3 to 2.5 centimetres high (smaller dimensions for the Dieulefit Picodon).

Things have changed since the days when every farmer's wife made a different sort of Picodon, and cheesemakers such as Monsieur Cavet, who owns the family-run 'affinerie' at Dieulefit, are very conscious of balancing traditional production with the stringent a.o.c. requirements. La Maison Cavet was established in 1920, at which time the 'coquetiers', the travelling grocers of the day, collected and sold on fruit, vegetable, eggs and 'fromages frais' from the farms.

The three Dieulefit cheesemakers of the day bought fresh cheeses from the coquetiers and then continued the process of turning them into Picodons. Nowadays, la Maison Cavet and other 'affineries' collect the two- or three-day old 'tommes fraîches' from most of the farmers who supply them, but the process is unchanged apart from modern hygiene requirements. The label of the 'affineurs' will state 'fermier' because the cheeses were started on the farms. Some farmers produce and market their own Picodons and these also carry the label 'fermier'. Other farmers send the milk to companies which make the cheeses and the labels from these companies will mention the 'laitier', the farmer who produced the milk.

There are standards for all aspects of Picodon production from goat to table and all those involved in the production have to meet these standards. Before a.o.c. status was granted in 1983, a Picodon affineur was fined for not showing on his labels which farm had started off each cheese – an impossible task.

Il y a ceux qui l'affinent, à Dieulefit et ailleurs, artisans du fromage amoureux du travail bien fait, les pieds dans l'histoire et la tête dans la modernité.

Manger du Picodon, c'est voyager un peu, sur les traces d'enfance ou le chemin des vacances.

Picodon rime avec passion
             Claire Chastan (Le Picodon; un fromage dans les étoiles)

There are the cheesemakers, in Dieulefit and round about, skilled workers in love with their craft, their feet in history and their heads in the modern world.

To eat a Picodon is to go travelling, along the pathways of childhood or holidays.

Picodon rhymes with pass-i-on.

The current regulations have had to take into account the practicalities of the way Picodons are produced, starting with the goats themselves, which must be given open grazing and, like Olympic athletes, no banned substances. Goats have had a chequered past in this forested, hilly, dry region where cows don't thrive. In 1231, the village of Valreas banned goats completely, because they were eating everything green, including the vines and the trees but, although the evidence suggests that they were tempted during various periods in the past, most communes stopped short of these drastic measures because the peasants would starve. Now goats are considered a positive part of conservation because they clear scrub and prevent fires, and it is a commonplace in Dieulefit to hear the goatbells, or even pass the herd as it is shepherded by two black and white collies from one part of the woods to another. No local fête is complete without its pen of goats, and three kids playing 'king of the castle' on a bale of straw.

Once the milk is collected, the cheesemaker adds a small amount of rennet (le présure) to the vat to induce curdling. This takes a couple of days and then the curds (le caillé) are strained from the whey ('le petit lait' or 'le sérum') into moulds ('moules') standing in a drainer. The cheeses are then drained and stood on racks to dry, a crucial stage in the process and one which nowadays uses mechanical ventilation. One reason that Dieulefit produced outstanding Picodons in the past was its 'good air', so famous that the village is still the French centre for research into respiratory problems. After drying, the Picodons are 'refined' ('affinés'), which is the stage that individual techniques make subtle changes to the taste and the appearance of the cheeses. Some cheesemakers prefer to create blueish rinds, others reddish; one wraps wet cloths around his maturing Picodons to create the desired effect . A Picodon must have matured for a fortnight – unless it is a Picodon méthode Dieulefit.

Legend says that a farmer living in Tonils at the foot of the Montagne de Couspeau forgot to put away a dish of goat's cheeses and when she found how hard they'd become, she thought she might rescue them by washing them in cold water. However it was discovered, it was the village of Dieulefit that gave its name to the process of washing Picodons, maturing them for at least a month and producing the smaller, stronger cheeses which for afficionados are the true Picodons.

Arguments about what makes a cheese a Picodon have not been ended by the a.o.c. regulations. These are quite clear as to the all-important 'terroir', the land where a Picodon can be produced (this can only be in the départements of la Drôme and l'Ardèche, or the two cantons of Barjac, in le Garde, and Valréas in le Vaucluse) and have prevented production of so-called Picodons as far away from their traditional home as Chile. However, controversy rages on and no two Picodons are alike. Poor quality Picodons taste soapy, metallic or even of potatoes; good picodons taste of goat 'caprine', and sting, 'piquent'. Everything else is a good topic for debate – over a glass of red Côtes de Rhone, the natural choice to accompany Picodons. 'Don't believe all the rubbish you read,' warn the staff at Cavet. 'We don't wash the cheeses in wine – or eau de vie – just good, plain water!

Dans ton lait écumant, soudain un tourbillon.
Un feu d'enfer, une tempête...
Le lait a disparu, il reste un picodon
Et sa saveur est une fête.

In your foaming milk a sudden whirlpool,
fires of hell, a tempest...
the milk all gone, a Picodon remains,
its taste a feast-day.

Dans ton lait écumant, il a tout conservé
Le panicaut, le miel, les asphyllantes,
Un rayon de soleil, une chanson d'été,
L'orage de l'enfer et la candeur des plantes.

In your foaming milk is everything
wild eryngo, honey, leafless flora
a ray of sun, a summer song
the storms of hell and honesty of plants.

Anonyme 1998, Taulignan

The tomme fraîche arrives at the *affinerie*

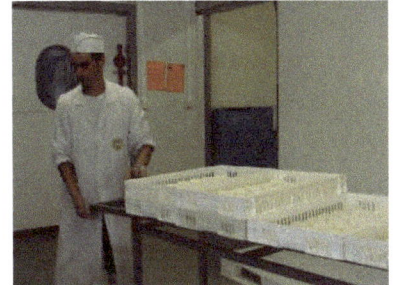

The name of the fermier who started the cheese is on the label

The Picodons mature on racks

Picodons méthode Dieulefit mature for at least 30 days and are repeatedly washed in water.

Cavet fille
and
Cavet fils

carry on the family business, keeping the best of the old ways amid the new technology.

I do like a little romance… just a sniff, as I call it, of the rocks and valleys… Of course, bread-and-cheese is the real thing. The rocks and valleys are no good at all, if you haven't got that.

Mrs Greenow in Anthony Trollope's 'Can you Forgive Her'

And as well as the various Picodon Festivals, there is France's most famous cross-country car rally, the **Dieulefit Picodon Rally**, which takes place in September each year. Spot the famous sponsors' names on the cars…

About the Author

Photo by Gary Martin

I'm a Welsh writer and photographer living in the south of France with a big white dog, a scruffy black dog, a Nikon D700 and a man. I taught English in Wales for many years and my claim to fame is that I was the first woman to be a secondary headteacher in Carmarthenshire. I'm mother or stepmother to five children so life has been pretty hectic.

I've published all kinds of books, both with conventional publishers and self-published. You'll find everything under my name from prize-winning poetry and novels, military history, translated books on dog training, to this cookery book on goat cheese. My passion for food photography started here and I've since had articles and photos published in journals and cookbooks.

My work with top dog-trainer Michel Hasbrouck has taken me deep into the world of dogs with problems, and inspired one of my novels. With Scottish parents, an English birthplace and French residence, I can usually support the winning team on most sporting occasions.

If you enjoyed this book, please leave a review on amazon, goodreads and/or wherever you bought the book, as this helps other readers to find it. If you're interested in my work or me, please read on.

If you liked my book, please help other readers find it by writing a review. Thank you.

Contact Jean Gill

I love to hear from readers. Email me at jean.gill@wanadoo.fr

Blog: news, views, tips and trivia at www.jeangill.blogspot.com where you can meet Sherlock, the abandoned hunting-dog we adopted.

Check out my website www.jeangill.com
My photos are for sale at www.istockphoto.com/portfolio/jeangillcom
Twitter @writerjeangill
Facebook www.facebook.com/writerjeangill

See my book trailers at www.youtube.com/user/beteljean

Recommendations, if you would like to read another book by Jean Gill:

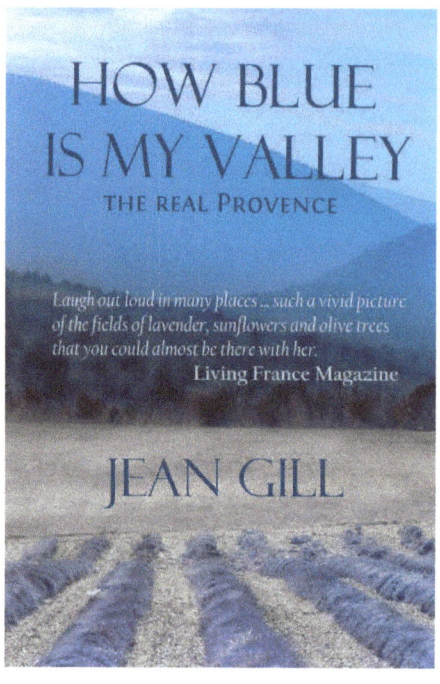

If you want to read more about my life in France, try *How Blue is my Valley*. Humorous travel/autobiography about my first year living in Provence and how it compared with Wales. Amazon UK No1 bestseller in 2013.

'Laugh out loud in many places... such a vivid picture of fields of lavender, sunflowers and olive trees that you could almost be there with her.' **Living France Magazine**

The true scents of Provence?
Lavender, thyme and septic tank.

How can you resist a village called Dieulefit, `God created it', the village 'where everyone belongs'. Discover the real Provence in good company ...

If you are a dog-lover, try *Someone to Look Up To*. Based on true stories. It's a dog's life in the south of France. From puppyhood, Sirius the Pyrenean Mountain Dog has been trying to understand his humans and train them with kindness...

How this led to divorce he has no idea. More misunderstandings take Sirius to Death Row in an animal shelter, as a so-called dangerous dog learning survival tricks from the other inmates. During the twilight barking, he is shocked to hear his brother's voice but the bitter-sweet reunion is short-lived. Doggedly, Sirius keeps the faith.

One day, his human will come.

This book gives a taste of the whole range of my writing and includes much that is autobiographical and even more than usual that is from the heart. You will know what I mean as you dip into this collection. If you want to read more about my life in France and a wide variety of short stories and poems, try *One Sixth of a Gill*.

'It will bring out emotions you never knew you had.' C.M.Stibbe, author of *The Fowler's Snare*

Five-minute reads.
Meet people you will never forget: the night photographer, the gynaecologist's wife, the rescue dog. Dip into whatever suits your mood, from comedy to murders; from fantastic stories to blog posts, by way of love poetry.

Fully illustrated by the author; Jean Gill's original photographs are as thought-provoking as her writing. An out of body experience for adventurous readers. Or, of course, you can *Live Safe*.

Not for you
the blind alley on a dark night,
wolf-lope pacing you step for step
as shadows flare on the walls.

If you like historical novels, try the winner of the Global Ebooks Award for Best Historical Fiction, *Song at Dawn.*

1150 in Provence, where love and marriage are as divided as Christian and Muslim.

A historical thriller set in Narbonne just after the Second Crusade. On the run from abuse, Estela wakes in a ditch with only her lute, her amazing voice, and a dagger hidden in her petticoats. Her talent finds a patron in Alienor of Aquitaine and more than a music tutor in the Queen's finest troubadour and Commander of the Guard, Dragonetz los Pros.

Weary of war, Dragonetz uses Jewish money and Moorish expertise to build that most modern of inventions, a papermill, arousing the wrath of the Church. Their enemies gather, ready to light the political and religious powder-keg of medieval Narbonne.

If you like romance, try *Snake on Saturdays.*
'Excellent and intelligent book about loss and healing.'
Leslie M Ficcaglia

Helen Tanner lives alone and likes it that way. She runs her own business, spends her evenings out with friends, and tries to think as little as possible about the tragedy she has left behind. Until, that is, a dark-haired vet walks into her shop and into her life.

Her first unpromising encounter with Llanelli vet Dai Evans turns into a tumultuous affair which brings about irrevocable changes for both of them. Dai becomes closer to his farming family, and helps them through the BSE crisis, while Helen is forced not only to consider a new future, but to face up to a troubled past.

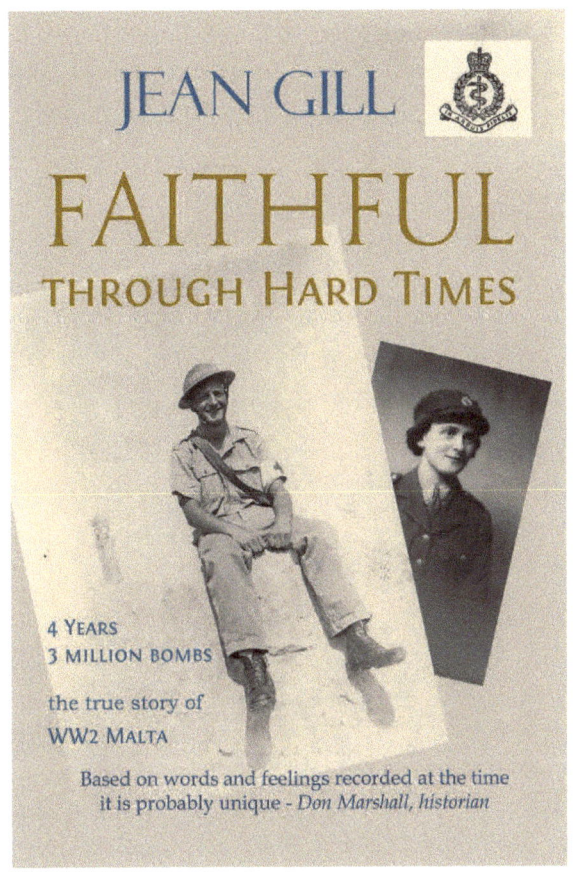

If you like biographies and true war stories, try *Faithful through Hard Times.*

'A most unusual military history book. There are few military non-combatant accounts of life in the Second World War, fewer still from an Other Rank. Based on words and feelings recorded at the time it is probably unique.' - Don Marshall, Military History Enthusiast

This is not a WW2 memoir. It is a riveting reconstruction from an eye-witness account written at the time in a secret diary, a diary too dangerous to show anyone and too precious to destroy.

The true story of four years, 3 million bombs, one small island out-facing the might of the German and Italian airforces - and one young Scotsman who didn't want to be there.

If you like Young Adult that works for adults too; if you're left-handed or know a leftie, try *On the Other Hand.*

A mix of gripping story with fascinating facts on left-handedness. Everyone should think left-handed - or so 14 year old Jamie thought when she tied her hand behind her back for a day-long protest in school, against persecution of left-handers over the centuries.

Her best friend Ryan publicised their cause with a new series of articles in the school magazine but just when their campaign is going well, Ryan's Mum drags him off from Wales to live in America. There he faces bullying at its most deadly and Jamie has to live from one email to the next to know whether her friend is coping.

Teachers' Resource materials available free from www.jeangill.com

INDEX